EARTH'S ENERGY EXPERIMENTS

SOLAR ENERGY
PROJECTS

Easy Energy Activities for
Future Engineers!

JESSIE ALKIRE

CONSULTING EDITOR, DIANE CRAIG, M.A./READING SPECIALIST

Super Sandcastle

An Imprint of Abdo Publishing
abdopublishing.com

abdopublishing.com

Published by Abdo Publishing, a division of ABDO, PO Box 398166, Minneapolis, Minnesota 55439. Copyright © 2019 by Abdo Consulting Group, Inc. International copyrights reserved in all countries. No part of this book may be reproduced in any form without written permission from the publisher. Super SandCastle™ is a trademark and logo of Abdo Publishing.

Printed in the United States of America, North Mankato, Minnesota
052018
092018

Design and Production: Mighty Media, Inc.
Editor: Liz Salzmann
Cover Photographs: iStockphoto; Mighty Media, Inc.
Interior Photographs: iStockphoto; Library of Congress; Mighty Media, Inc.; Shutterstock

The following manufacturers/names appearing in this book are trademarks: Kerr®, KitchenAid®, LEGO®, Market Pantry™, Morton®, Plaid® Mod Podge®, Scotch®, Sharpie®

Library of Congress Control Number: 2017961711

Publisher's Cataloging-in-Publication Data
Names: Alkire, Jessie, author.
Title: Solar energy projects: Easy energy activities for future engineers! / by Jessie Alkire.
Other titles: Easy energy activities for future engineers!
Description: Minneapolis, Minnesota : Abdo Publishing, 2019. | Series: Earth's energy experiments
Identifiers: ISBN 9781532115653 (lib.bdg.) | ISBN 9781532156373(ebook)
Subjects: LCSH: Solar energy--Juvenile literature. | Handicraft--Juvenile literature. | Science projects--Juvenile literature. | Electricity--Experiments--Juvenile literature.
Classification: DDC 621.47--dc23

Super SandCastle™ books are created by a team of professional educators, reading specialists, and content developers around five essential components—phonemic awareness, phonics, vocabulary, text comprehension, and fluency—to assist young readers as they develop reading skills and strategies and increase their general knowledge. All books are written, reviewed, and leveled for guided reading and early reading intervention programs for use in shared, guided, and independent reading and writing activities to support a balanced approach to literacy instruction.

TO ADULT HELPERS

The projects in this title are fun and simple. There are just a few things to remember to keep kids safe. Some projects require the use of sharp or hot objects. Also, kids may be using messy materials such as glue or paint. Make sure they protect their clothes and work surfaces. Review the projects before starting, and be ready to assist when necessary.

KEY SYMBOLS

Watch for these warning symbols in this book. Here is what they mean.

HOT!
You will be working with something hot. Get help!

SHARP!
You will be working with a sharp object. Get help!

CONTENTS

What Is Solar Energy?   **4**

Using Solar Energy for Electricity   **6**

Using Solar Energy for Heat   **8**

Materials   **10**

Solar Panel Color Test   **12**

Solar Oven S'mores   **14**

Updraft Tower   **18**

Solar Salt Remover   **22**

Fairy Light Lantern   **24**

Simple Solar Fan   **26**

Conclusion   **30**

Quiz   **31**

Glossary   **32**

WHAT IS SOLAR ENERGY?

Solar energy is energy from the sun. Sunlight is the largest source of energy on Earth. It is made up of **radiation**. This radiation can be converted into heat or electricity.

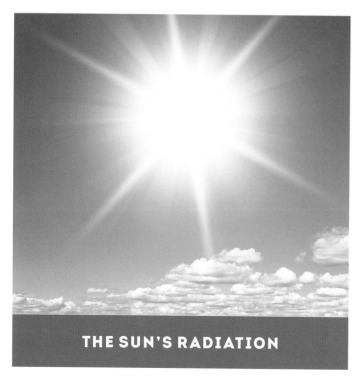

THE SUN'S RADIATION

Solar energy is a growing **resource**. It is popular because it is renewable. This means it **replaces** itself naturally. Solar energy is also a clean energy. It does not pollute the air.

However, converting and storing solar energy is very costly. And it requires the use of solar cells. Solar **panels** are made up of many solar cells. This means solar panels can take up a lot of space. Scientists are working on solving this problem.

SOLAR PANELS ON A ROOF

USING SOLAR ENERGY FOR ELECTRICITY

Solar energy is often converted into electricity. This electricity can power something as small as a watch or as large as a **satellite**!

SOLAR CELL HISTORY

Solar cells convert solar energy into electricity. Solar cells are also called photovoltaic cells. The first ones that worked well were created in 1954.

Since then, solar cells have improved greatly. Today, solar cells can power anything from a garden light to a whole house!

MODERN SOLAR CELL LIGHT

HOW SOLAR CELLS WORK

A solar cell has two main layers. The layers are made of two **semiconductors**. One is **negative** and the other is **positive**. Sunlight shines on the solar cell. Energy from the light is **transferred** to loose electrons in the negative semiconductor. This causes the electrons to move from the negative conductor to the positive conductor and back. This continuous movement of electrons is the electrical current.

A solar cell can be connected to a load, such as a light bulb. This creates an electrical circuit. The electricity from the solar cell travels to the light bulb and back. This turns on the light!

A single solar cell only creates a small amount of electricity. But many solar cells are often connected to make solar **panels**. Solar panels can create a lot of electricity.

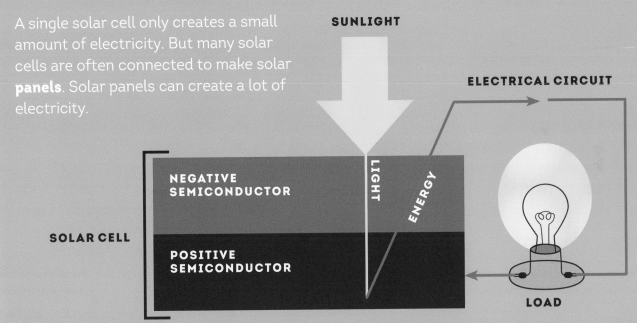

SUNLIGHT

ELECTRICAL CIRCUIT

LIGHT

ENERGY

NEGATIVE SEMICONDUCTOR

SOLAR CELL

POSITIVE SEMICONDUCTOR

LOAD

USING SOLAR ENERGY FOR HEAT

Solar energy can also be converted to heat. In fact, people have been using the sun as a heat source for centuries!

HEAT HISTORY

People first used simple methods to heat their homes with the sun's energy. They built houses with large windows. The windows allowed a lot of sunlight to come in and heat the homes.

Nearly 1,000 years ago, Anasazi Native Americans used solar energy. They built homes in cliffs that faced south. This meant the homes would get more heat from the sun.

ANASAZI CLIFF SETTLEMENT, MESA VERDE NATIONAL PARK, COLORADO

MARIA TELKES

Maria Telkes was a scientist. She was born in Budapest, Hungary, in 1900. In 1924, Telkes moved to the United States. She worked for the Solar Energy Conversion Project at the Massachusetts Institute of Technology. In 1948, Telkes **designed** and built the first home heated by solar energy from solar collectors. Telkes became well-known for her work with solar energy.

SOLAR HEAT TODAY

Modern solar collectors capture solar energy and convert it to heat. Many solar collectors are large, flat metal plates. Some are made up of rows of tubes.

A solar collector is connected to a heating system inside a building. The sun heats a liquid inside the collector. The warm liquid flows to the heating system for use as heat. The heat energy can be used immediately or stored for later use.

SOLAR COLLECTORS ON A ROOF

MATERIALS

Here are some of the materials that you will need for the projects in this book.

ALUMINUM FOIL **CAN OPENER** **CARD STOCK** **CRAFT KNIFE** **CRAFT STICKS**

DC MOTOR **DOUBLE-SIDED TAPE** **DUCT TAPE** **FOOD COLORING** **GRAHAM CRACKERS**

HOT GLUE GUN & GLUE STICKS

LARGE MARSHMALLOWS

LEGO BRICKS

MASKING TAPE

MASON JAR

MOD PODGE MATTE

NEEDLE-NOSE PLIERS

PLASTIC FAN PROPELLER

PLASTIC WRAP

SHOE BOX WITH ATTACHED LID

SOLAR FAIRY LIGHT INSERT

SOLDERING IRON & SOLDER

WIRE

WIRE CUTTER

WIRE STRIPPER

SOLAR PANEL COLOR TEST

MATERIALS: cardboard, ruler, marker, scissors, newspaper, paint (black, white & 4 other colors), paintbrushes, 8 × 12-inch baking pan, 6 ice cubes, notebook, pencil

Do you know what the best color for a solar **panel** is? Find out which colors take in the most heat with this experiment!

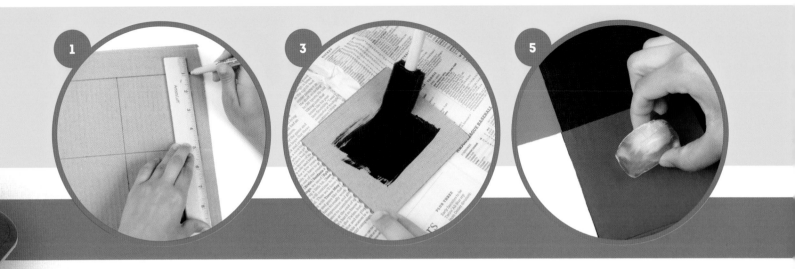

① Draw six 4-inch (10 cm) squares on cardboard. Cut them out.

② Cover your work surface with newspaper.

③ Paint each square a different color. Paint one square black and one square white. Paint the other four squares any colors you want! Let the paint dry.

④ Place the cardboard squares in the pan.

⑤ Place one ice cube on each cardboard square. Make sure the ice cubes are the same size!

⑥ Place the pan in direct sunlight.

⑦ Observe the ice cubes. Which color's ice cube melted the fastest? Which one melted the slowest?

⑧ Record the results in a notebook.

SOLAR OVEN S'MORES

MATERIALS: newspaper, shoe box with attached lid, ruler, marker, craft knife, black paint, paintbrush, aluminum foil, double-sided tape, plastic wrap, wooden skewer (optional), graham crackers, large marshmallows, chocolate bar

People have used solar ovens for almost 200 years. These devices reflect sunlight to heat and cook food. Some people still use solar ovens today!

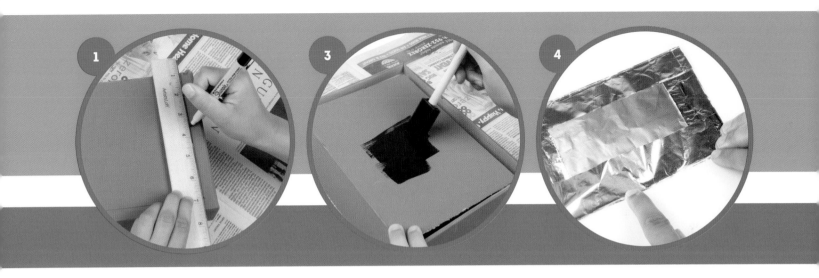

1 Cover your work surface with newspaper. Set the shoe box on the newspaper. Draw a line along the front and each side of the lid. The lines should be ½ inch (1.3 cm) in from the edges.

2 Have an adult help you cut along the lines with a craft knife. This creates a flap.

3 Paint the box black. Let the paint dry.

4 Fold pieces of aluminum foil the same sizes as the bottom and each side of the box. Make sure the shiny side of the foil is facedown.

Continued on the next page.

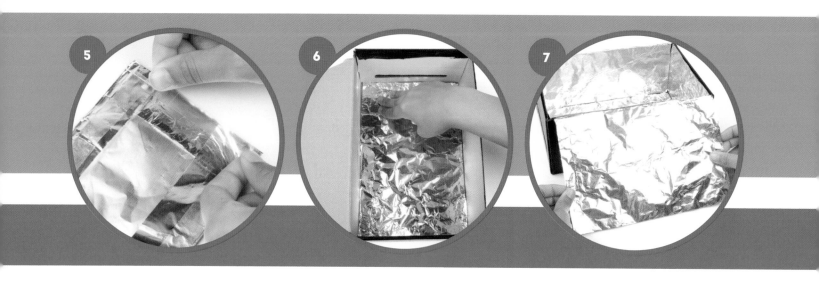

5 Put double-sided tape around the edges of the foil pieces.

6 Tape the foil pieces inside the box. Try to keep the foil as flat and even as possible. The shiny sides should now be facing up.

7 Fold a piece of foil the size of the flap. Use double-sided tape to tape it to the inside of the flap. Tape it with the shiny side facing up.

8 Raise the flap. Cover the box's opening with plastic wrap. Make sure the wrap is as smooth and tight as possible.

9 Set the oven outside so the sun shines into it. If necessary, prop up the flap with a wooden skewer. Wait 30 minutes for the oven to preheat.

10 Place graham cracker squares on a piece of foil.

11 Place a marshmallow on each graham cracker. Carefully pull the plastic wrap back. Place the crackers inside the oven.

12 **Replace** the plastic wrap tightly. Make sure the flap is still open. Leave the oven in the sun for one hour or until the marshmallows are soft.

13 Pull the plastic wrap back. Place a square of chocolate on each marshmallow. Replace the plastic wrap.

14 Leave the oven in the sun until the chocolate melts.

15 Remove the s'mores from the oven. Complete them by topping each one with another graham cracker square.

UPDRAFT TOWER

MATERIALS: 3 empty soup cans, can opener, newspaper, black paint, paintbrush, duct tape, thick & thin wire, ruler, wire cutter, pushpin, needle-nose pliers, card stock, marker, scissors, clear tape, 2 books that are the same thickness

Sunlight can cause the air to move. This happens when the sun heats the air near the ground. Then the hot air rises above the cooler air. This is called an updraft.

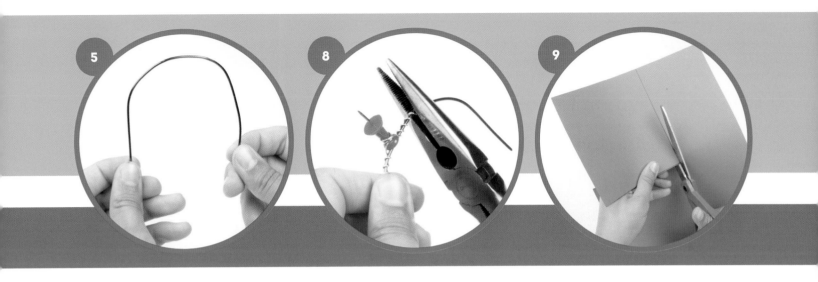

① Have an adult help you remove the bottoms of the soup cans with a can opener.

② Cover your work surface with newspaper. Paint the cans black. Let the paint dry.

③ Tape the cans together so they form a tall tower.

④ Cut a 6-inch (15 cm) piece of thick wire.

⑤ Bend the wire to form an arch.

⑥ Cut a 6-inch (15 cm) piece of thin wire.

⑦ Wrap the middle of the thin wire twice around the pushpin.

⑧ Use a pliers to twist the ends of the thin wire around the thick wire. The pushpin should point up from the center of the arch.

⑨ Cut a 5-inch (13 cm) square out of card stock.

Continued on the next page.

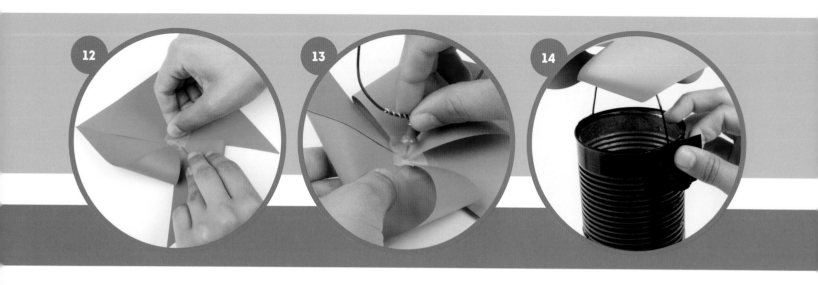

(10) Make a mark in the center of the square.

(11) Cut in from each corner of the square. Stop cutting ¼ inch (0.6 cm) from the center mark.

(12) Tape every other point to the center mark. Do not fold them flat. This makes a pinwheel!

(13) Poke the pushpin through center of the pinwheel.

(14) Tape the ends of the arched wire to the top of the can tower.

(15) Place the books near a window in direct sunlight. Set the tower on the books. Center it on the space between the books.

(16) Observe the tower. The sun warms the air inside the tower. The air rises. The rising air causes the pinwheel to spin!

A new kind of solar power plant uses a solar updraft tower. This is a tall tower in the middle of a collector. The collector is a low, wide structure with a clear roof. The sun heats the air in the collector. The hot air moves into and up the tower. As the air enters the tower, it flows through **turbines**. The turbines spin, which powers a **generator** that creates electricity.

One advantage of a solar updraft tower is that it doesn't need constant sunlight to work. It can even work at night! This is because the ground stores enough heat during the day to keep the air in the collector warm overnight.

SOLAR
UPDRAFT
TOWER

TURBINE

SUNLIGHT

SUNLIGHT

COLLECTOR

GENERATOR

AIRFLOW

SOLAR SALT REMOVER

MATERIALS: measuring cup, warm tap water, medium bowl, salt, spoon, large glass bowl, ruler, small bowl, plastic wrap, masking tape, a weight such as a rock

Solar energy can be used to remove salt from saltwater! This process is called distilling. The sun's heat causes saltwater to **evaporate** and **condense**. This removes the salt and cleans the water. The device used to distill saltwater is called a solar still.

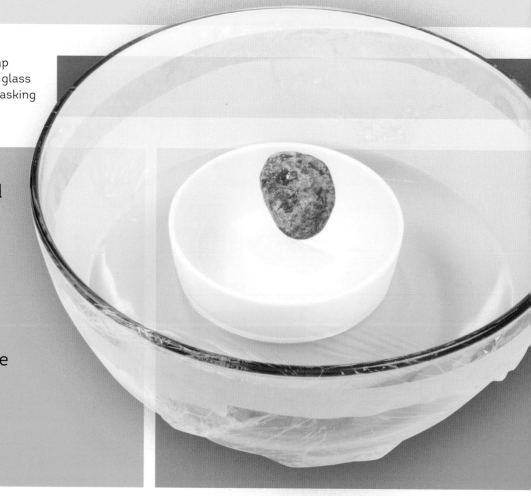

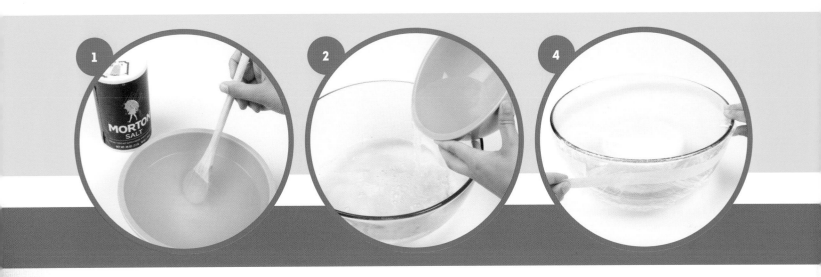

1. Pour about 3 cups of warm water into a bowl. Add ½ cup of salt. Stir until the salt **dissolves**.

2. Pour the saltwater into a large glass bowl. It should be about 2 inches (5 cm) deep.

3. Place a small empty bowl in the large bowl. The top of the small bowl should be higher than the level of the saltwater.

4. Cover the large bowl with plastic wrap. Make it as smooth and tight as you can. Tape the plastic wrap in place.

5. Place a weight on the plastic wrap. Make sure the weight is centered above the small bowl.

6. Place the bowl outside in a spot that gets sunlight most of the day.

7. Leave the solar still for at least a day. The longer you leave it, the more water you'll distill!

8. Remove the plastic wrap. Measure how much water collected in the small bowl.

9. Taste the water from the small bowl. Is it salty? Or does it taste like normal tap water?

FAIRY LIGHT LANTERN

MATERIALS: solar fairy light insert, bowl, measuring spoon, water, food coloring, spoon, mason jar, Mod Podge Matte, 5 craft sticks, newspaper, ribbon, scissors, hot glue gun & glue sticks

Some devices, such as lights, run on solar-powered batteries. To work, these devices need to sit in the sun. The solar energy charges the batteries. Once charged, the batteries can power the device!

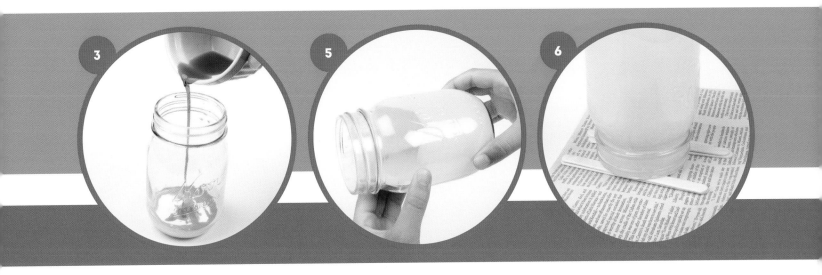

① Place the solar fairy light insert in direct sunlight to charge it.

② Put a tablespoon of water in a small bowl. Stir in a few drops of food coloring.

③ Put 2 tablespoons of Mod Podge in the mason jar. Add the colored water. Stir well with a craft stick.

④ Cover your work surface with newspaper. Set two craft sticks next to each other. Place two more craft sticks on top of the first two.

⑤ Turn the jar to coat the inside with the Mod Podge mixture.

⑥ Set the jar upside down on the craft sticks to dry.

⑦ Cut a piece of ribbon to make a handle. Hot glue the ends of the ribbon to the sides of the jar's lid.

⑧ **Replace** the center part of the lid with the solar fairy light insert. Make sure the solar cell faces out the top of the lid. Turn on the fairy lights. Screw the lid onto the jar.

SIMPLE SOLAR FAN

MATERIALS: DC motor, wire stripper, 2.5w solar panel, soldering iron, solder, LEGO basic bricks, large LEGO plate, hot glue gun & glue sticks, small plastic fan propeller

Solar **panels** create electricity. This electricity can then power a motor. Solar-powered motors can spin fans, move toy cars, and more!

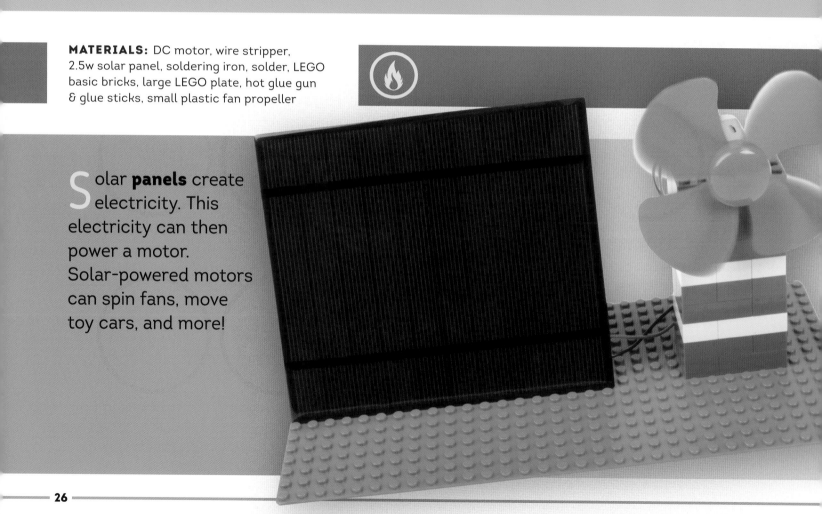

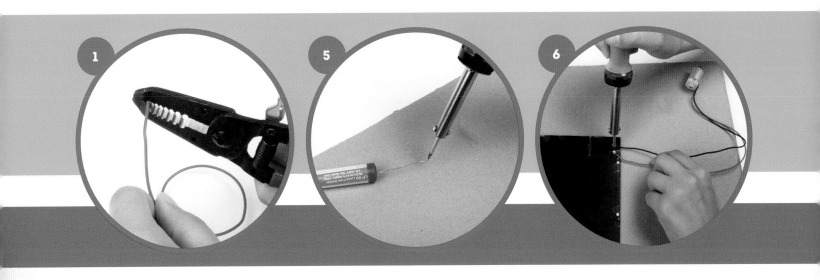

① Strip ½ inch (1.3 cm) of coating off the ends of the DC motor's wires.

② Set the solar **panel** facedown. Set the DC motor next to it.

③ Line up the motor's **positive** wire with the solar panel's positive **soldering** point.

④ Line up the motor's **negative** wire with the solar panel's negative soldering point.

⑤ Have an adult help you load the soldering iron with solder. Follow the directions that came with the soldering iron.

⑥ Solder the wires to the solar panel.

Continued on the next page.

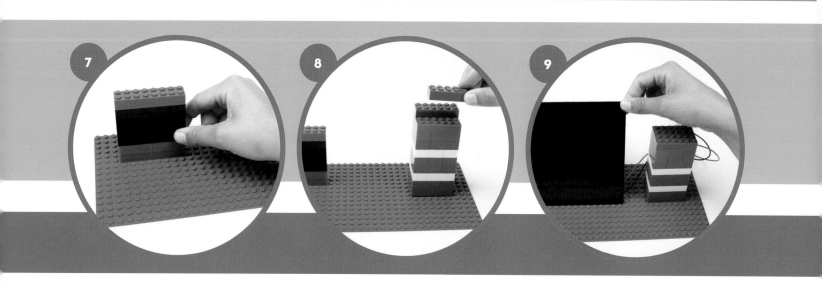

7 Make a LEGO tower that is seven bricks tall. Connect the tower to the LEGO plate near one corner.

8 Build a second LEGO tower on the other side of the plate. Make it a few bricks taller than the first tower.

9 Lean the solar **panel** against the first tower.

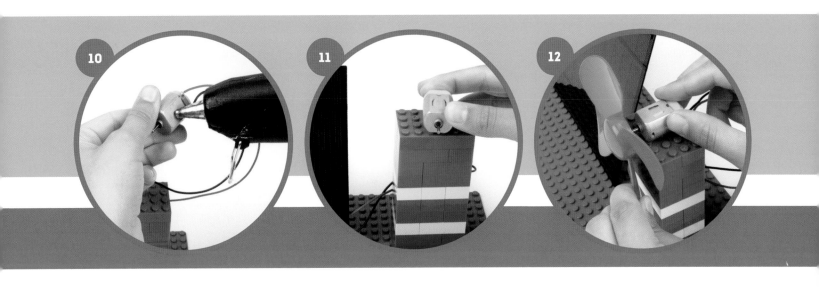

10 Put a large dot of hot glue on the bottom of the motor.

11 Stick the motor to the top of the second tower. The motor shaft should face forward.

12 Place the hole in the propeller onto the motor's shaft.

13 Place your solar fan in direct sunlight. Watch it spin!

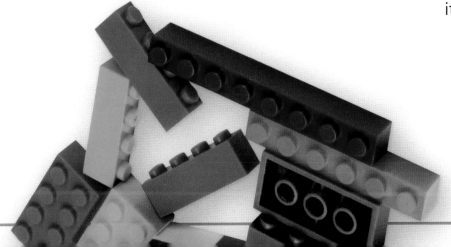

CONCLUSION

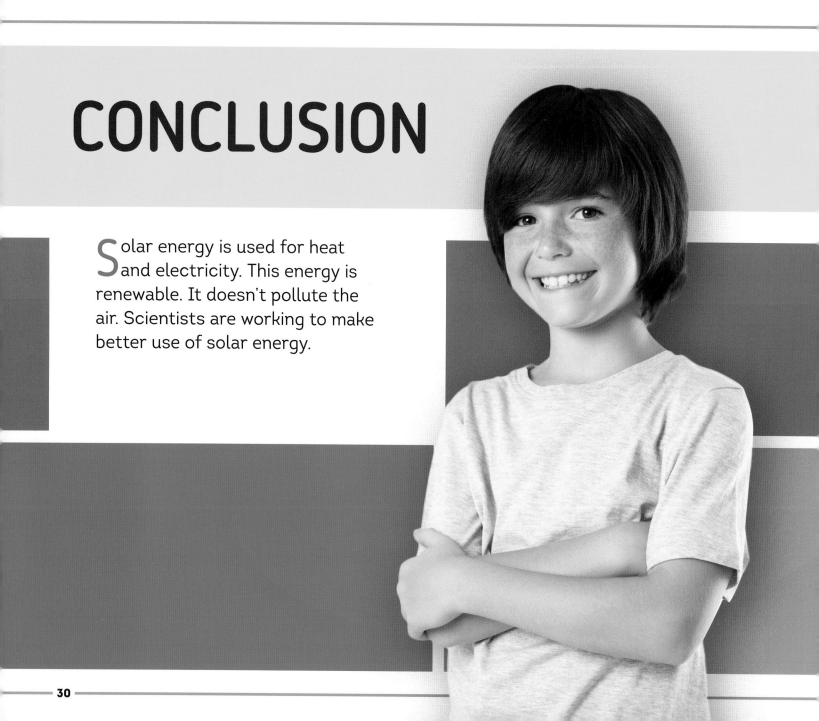

Solar energy is used for heat and electricity. This energy is renewable. It doesn't pollute the air. Scientists are working to make better use of solar energy.

QUIZ

1. Solar energy is a renewable **resource**. TRUE OR FALSE?

2. What does a solar cell convert solar energy into?

3. Who **designed** and built the first solar-heated home using solar collectors?

LEARN MORE ABOUT IT!

You can find out more about solar energy at the library. Or you can ask an adult to help you **research** solar energy on the internet!

Answers: 1. True   2. Electricity   3. Maria Telkes

GLOSSARY

condense – to change from a gas into a liquid or a solid.

design – to plan how something will appear or work.

dissolve – to become part of a liquid.

evaporate – to change from a liquid into a gas.

generator – a machine that creates electricity.

negative – related to a wire or connector that energy flows toward when used in a circuit.

panel – part of a flat surface.

positive – related to a wire or connector that energy flows away from when used in a circuit.

radiation – energy from the sun.

replace – 1. to take the place of something. 2. to put something back where it was.

research – to find out more about something.

resource – something that is usable or valuable.

satellite – a man-made object that orbits Earth.

semiconductor – a material or object that allows some electricity or heat to move through it.

solder – a mixture of metals that is melted and used to join metal parts together. To solder is to connect or repair something using solder.

transfer – to pass from one thing or place to another.

turbine – a machine that produces power when it is rotated at high speed.